TURNING PAGES OF MY LIFE

SAMUEL NISBETT

Copyright © 2024 SAMUEL NISBETT

All rights reserved.

DEDICATION

To,

Gladys Maynard

Brenda Moore

Erna Roth

Dr. Rev S Rays Blake

And to you, if you have stuck with Sam till the very end.

Contents

DEDICATION i

CHAPTER 1 IN THE BEGINNING 3

CHAPTER 2 TEEN REBEL 11

CHAPTER 3 CHAOS 25

CHAPTER 4 NAVIGATION 32

CHAPTER 5 DELETED 38

CHAPTER 6 SEARCHING 46

CHAPTER 7 I AM NOT TIRED YET 56

CHAPTER 8 THANKS 60

CHAPTER ONE
IN THE BEGINNING

No work so great, but what admits decay,
No act so glorious, but must fade away...
Old things must yield to new, common to strange,
Perpetual motion, brings perpetual change.

— *James Miller*

I grew up in a strict household. As a child, God and religion were shoved down my throat, stuffing me entirely. This didn't leave room for me to think of anything else. It wasn't exactly terrible, but the persuasion of the act felt like overkill. I always thought that religion should be something sacred and personal. However, it was organized and scheduled as if God was on a certain timeline. I agreed with my family for a time, but age is a funny thing. We learn, and we grow. We become more critical. I didn't stay complacent for long: eventually, I had to empty myself out of everything that was taught to me.

My mother was Olive Hendrickson before she met my father. She was born on March 24, 1930, in Cuba. She had a big family; she was the sixth of ten children. She learned how to embroider and sew at an early age. The woman was remarkably talented with nimble fingers and a quick wit. She was also terrifying.

When she was fifteen, she moved to the United States to live with her aunt. This was a turning point for her. She met the love of her life, my father, a few years after she came from Cuba. He was born in Harlem. Their love was hasty, instantaneous, and it made sense back then. Eldridge Nisbett and Olive were married in November 1949. My mother went through a life-changing experience in 1954: she met Jesus Christ and was filled with the Holy Spirit. Eldridge and Olive were living in the Bronx at this time. She became Sister Olive and joined the church of *Youth Mission of Life* with her husband. The woman was a powerhouse, and the Holy Spirit ruled her life… and the lives of her children.

I was the youngest child of my parents. There were two brothers and a sister who came before me, and I was raised under their care, as well as my parents' watchful gaze. I was always looked after, advised, and loved. The way I see it, I had three fathers and two mothers, more than most people have in their lifetimes. I remember being lulled to sleep by my sister, my brothers calming me down after I scraped my knee, my mother kissing my forehead when I washed up for dinner, and my father taking us camping.

I remember being safe for a time in my childhood home.

My family, bless them, always wanted the best for me. But I do feel like they were too hard on me. Despite the coddling and affection, I was suffocated by their ideals and values. My parents were firm and set in their rules. My mother, especially, believed in tough love. Her motto was, "My way or the highway." We learned this the hard way and adhered to it. I became accustomed to my mother's anger. It transformed, changing shape and size depending on the day or her mood. It developed as I grew older and more defiant, taking the form of abuse. Her words were visceral sharp and loud, heavy with disdain. I could feel the wrath as she hurled abuses my way, and I could feel a horrible emotion festering inside me.

One of her favorite verses was from Ruth 1:16. It said, "Thy people shall be my people, and thy God my God." This did not apply when my family was making me feel worthless. It did not apply when it should have.

My mother was a lion. She would dress me in raggedy clothes with the pants ripped. They made me look like a hobo. I had to sit at the back of the church, which was called hobo lane. I remember my church friend had to sit in hobo lane on Thanksgiving for misbehaving. He was given an empty dog food bowl while everyone else, including myself, ate delicious food and dressed nice. I remember feeling really sad for him, but I was glad it wasn't me this time.

My mother wanted people to know that I had messed up, and she wanted me to understand its consequences. Sometimes, as a punishment, she would make me pray all night on my knees to teach me a lesson. It wasn't terrible. It was fear. My parents feared the church, and they feared what would happen if they didn't raise their kids in the right way of the church. They didn't want to get into trouble. But I was traumatized... so I rebelled.

She loved me: I was her youngest, her baby boy. But she also loved the church and what it taught. She was a woman of God first and a mother second. She watched me become harder with each passing day. My siblings never turned against my parents, they wouldn't have dared, and I became the black sheep. I became stubborn, and my mother's abuse didn't bother me much. I stood out from my family like a sore thumb, and a saddening distance was created between us.

My father was not aggressive the way my mother was. While our family operated on set rules and models, my father remained calm and mellow. He was a preacher and very God-fearing. He worked as a head baker for thirty-two years on Rikers Island, one of the most notorious prisons in the US. It was one of the places I never wanted to go to. He chastised us, sure, but my mother had the harder hand. I don't blame my parents for what they did. They were ruled by fear, by the church, and it was a powerful tool. I don't like using the word 'abuse' (although I am told that it is applicable), and I prefer thinking my parents did what they thought was best. My mother would often warn me that she would send me to Cuba whenever I was acting out. I believe that they were fed false evidence. It appears real, especially when fear is instilled.

The leadership of the church ex-communicated me when I was twelve. Even when I left the church, there was a lingering fear inside me that something would go wrong. I had nothing but the streets. So, yes, it led me straight to Rikers Island in the long run.

I do have some fond memories from my childhood. When we were younger, we used to go to my Aunt Tilly and Uncle Kelly's place for New Year's Eve. When we entered the building, we could smell the chitlins. To me, that smelled like Christmas, and I never knew what it was until later on in life.

We were allowed to relax a bit, eat holiday food and watch TV with our cousins. My parents would monitor us closely, my mother's right eye twitching incessantly, but it wasn't their house. The food was amazing there, and I loved my aunt: she was like my mother but calmer. It was peaceful in their house, especially when it was cold outside, and we were supposed to huddle close together in the living room. I could listen to music over there, a luxury I was not awarded at my own house.

My father used to take us camping. When we woke up, we would all have to go looking for our shoes in the morning. He was playful like that. He used to take out our shoes and throw them at the raccoons, trying to keep us safe. But then we had to go find them like it was a game. It was a lot of fun.

I had fun with my brothers. They liked to tickle me because they thought it was funny. But sometimes I started crying, and it wasn't fun anymore. I was the youngest, so when they got their ten-speed bikes, I got a banana seat bike. I couldn't go on long bike rides with them. I always felt left out, so I tried to make my own way, and I fell away from them.

Growing up in the Bronx, we were surrounded by animals. My brother had a lot of lizards; he liked to keep them as pets. We also had a monkey called Getlow. He was a squirrel monkey, and we adored him. At the same time, we had a black lavender retriever called Jack. Jack hated that all the attention went to the monkey and (this sounds funny) he ran away. The dog ran away because he was jealous! We looked all over The Bronx for this dog, but we never managed to find him.

Time passed, and I became more and more rebellious. As a kid, sometimes I would skip school with my friends. We would go to Macy's instead. We would steal the AFX slot cars well into the afternoon until a security guard caught us one day. We were told not to come back without our parents. One time, I went to the mall with my sister. My sister went into Macy's, and I was scared to meet that guard there. I didn't want to get into trouble. But I never saw that man again.

I was part of a gang. We called ourselves *The Bloody Angels*. We were troublemakers, strutting along the streets as if we were powerful men. My parents were told about my activities, and it worried them. They tried to reason with me. I did not listen.

By the time I was eleven years old, I was more troubled than before. My family tolerated me to some extent, but I was getting out of hand. I skipped school more often. I drank and smoked, and I joined a gang. I was smoking Winchesters back then. The way I was able to get money for this was funny. My mother used to give me candy money, and I used to steal candy across the street from my elementary school. Then, I would tell the man at the store that I was buying cigarettes for my mother. They always went for it. This was just the start of my journey.

At the age of twelve, I was already shooting guns. I was exiled from church. I didn't understand it. I was a kid. The trauma became a part of me, and I became worse.

My mom figured it out eventually, and she had to make a difficult decision. My parents decided to buy a home in Hartsdale.

My whole family moved there because they were trying to bring me to a better neighborhood. So, we prepared for the move to Hartsdale, New York.

The move was a shock for me. Hartsdale was predominantly white, and I didn't think I could fit in. It was rough, but my parents were trying to make a better home for me. They wanted to get me away from the city and give me a chance.

CHAPTER TWO
TEEN REBEL

Some of your children's rebellion against your spiritual lifestyle might be a necessary step in their finding an authentic relationship with God. But beware: If they find it, it might look quite different from what you've always thought it should be.

— Tim Kimmel

My parents thought it was good for a kid like me to have an outlet. I was put in gymnastics training when I was twelve. My mother told me that she hoped gymnastics would help me figure out who I was: in terms of my ideas and body. I thought she was being ridiculous but went to the classes anyway. *Anything to get out of the house*, I thought. The classes were strenuous but fun. I enjoyed my time there, but it did not bring me closer to God or to my family. I listened to the music that the other children listened to on the bus ride, and I liked the beat of every song. Music was freeing and soulful. Only church music was allowed in my house. Anything else would drive my parents mad.

During this time, my parents went to the shelter and adopted a St. Bernard. They're big, fun-loving dogs. The St. Bernard was for my brothers and me, and my sister got a Toy Poodle. We would take both dogs out, and people looked at us funny. I remember taking them to the field nearby the Catholic school. The big dog saw a squirrel, and I knew it stood no chance. He caught it but didn't kill it. He just threw it in the air a couple of times and then let it go. But I remember how happy he was. He had finally caught a squirrel! It was pretty exciting for me… and for him.

At this point in life, I didn't really deal with my brothers. But I wanted to have a relationship with them. I had a situation at school. This guy was messing with me and I was fed up with it. So, I told him one day, "I'm going home, getting my brother, and coming back for you." I knew I couldn't get my brother, but I could get the St. Bernard. My dog was playful, but people didn't see that. They were afraid of his size. They would see me coming, his leash in hand, and they'd run the other way.

I brought the dog to school, and I said to him, "Go get him!" And my dog, bless him, he was so excited. He started chasing that kid. But he was only playing. It was funny, the guy ran like a madman, but my dog kept chasing him.

The guy never bothered me again.

I worked hard for my money but had to do it illegally on the streets by selling drugs and stolen items. This is what I wanted to be: a street hustler.

I was a young African-American boy, enjoying my new neighborhood, and making new connections. I wanted to do more with my life, away from the influence of the church and my parents. It was during this time that I became friends with Alan Ross. Alan was the best. He was positive and kind. We were a good team, despite our differences. He was my neighbor. We used to build treehouses and forts together. We went into the landscaping business together at twelve years old! We would cut lawns and make money. We even bought our own lawnmower from our profits. His mother was a potter, and we helped her set up her shows. Fifty-one years later, Alan and I are still best friends.

I had no fear, and I went for what I wanted. I would sell weed to teenagers after church, and I wanted to represent the Bronx. I was operating in the streets, confident and strong, unwavering. I stopped going to church when my business saw profits, and I made a name for myself.

When we lived in Hartsdale, my parents would still drive the family to church. Sometimes they left me at home. I had this fort in the woods, and my friends would come over and hang out. We smoked weed and partied, deep into the woods, in our hiding spot. One day, my family was at church, and I was sitting on the porch. Some of my friends stopped by and asked if I wanted to smoke. So, we smoked in the house. And I don't know what happened, but word got out that I was having a party. Suddenly, all these kids were over at my house. We started partying. As luck would have it, that day, only that day, my parents came back early.

My mother was fuming. She flung the kids out of the house, yelling at them. I hid away in the basement and snuck out. I didn't go back home for two weeks. I lived in the fort, in the woods. My friend Liz used to bring me food. When everyone was at work or at school, I snuck back into the house to take a shower. I would eat breakfast too. And my mother knew; she knew I was coming around and eating her food. Eggs would be missing, and I made a mess sometimes. She tried to catch up with me a couple of times, but my friends were on the watch.

I didn't get caught. And my friends and I continued to party in the woods like always.

I eventually came back home. Now, when my family went to church, I had to go with them. But I had to sit in the car. I waited until church ended because I was no longer welcome there. While sitting in the car, waiting for my family, I got into more mischief. I found ways to buy my first drugs to smoke and sell. I bought a nickel bag of marijuana that was five blocks away from the church at this spot called the red door. When my family and I drove home I was so high that I thought I saw six lanes on the highway instead of three.

I was sent to sleepaway camps when my parents wanted me out of the house. They hoped it would take me away from my gang and my devilish activities. So, a growing strapping young boy was shipped off whenever it was convenient. I went for a few years, happy to be away from the house. But I didn't change my ways.

I ended up hooking up with a girl the third year and in my cabin, of all places! After that, we sneaked to the woods with some other kids and started smoking weed. I got caught, and they called my mother and father to get me. They were disappointed, and we didn't talk during the hour-long car ride back home. I watched them drive me home in the night, my mother's eyebrows furrowed with worry, my father's hands gripping the steering wheel. I was humiliated. I loved them more in that moment than I ever did after.

When I got home, I wanted to go see my new girl. I had no money, but I did have weed, so I decided to hitchhike to Connecticut. I made it to the Merritt Parkway and got stopped by the police. When the policeman asked what was in my pocket, I said, "Socks."

When I emptied my pocket, it was a bag of weed. The policeman said he could arrest me for it. I was only a teenager but I was trafficking weed from state to state, which was a very big crime. I was shaken like a leaf but thank God for my guardian angel. The policeman told me he didn't want to do any more paperwork and to get out of there. I started running but he made me come back. I was scared.

He went, "What do you think I'm gonna do with this?"

He was talking about the weed apparently. He told me to take it. "I don't want it," he said and gave me my eighty-five cents and my big bag of weed.

That day I had to stay in a little hallway, waiting for the morning. As the sun rose, I saw a couple of construction workers and sold them a few joints of weed. I made it to Connecticut to meet my new girlfriend. Boy, at that time I still didn't know what love was all about at least I thought it was love.

I was only allowed to listen to religious music in the house I was in. But when I went over to my Aunt Rita's, I used to love to hear the 107.5 WBLS urban adult FM NY radio station. That was a true treat for me.

My friends and I were into rock and roll. We used to listen to Pink Floyd and Genesis. I was the only African American kid in our group, just a little chocolate boy, and while it was a unique experience, my friends and I didn't see color. Not back then. So, we had five tickets to go to this Grateful Dead concert. There were four of us, and my friend Scott and I decided to hitchhike there. It was eighty-two miles from Hartsdale to New Jersey. We went all the way to English Town in Jersey. We were fifteen years old, on the highway, and we stood on the side of the road and put our thumbs out. We had a little sign that said, "Free ticket to the Dead."

We were very young and immature. Scott had very long hair. We both had bandanas on, and at the back of our shirts was the band's name.

So, this Spanish guy picked us up. He asked us, "Hey, what's the Dead?"

And we laughed and said, "The rock group."

He went, "I wish I could go. But I can give you a ride part way."

He brought us to the Bronx. It was a rough area, and two little kids were in the middle of it. Even though I was from the area, I was freaked out. We continued to hitchhike until a car stopped by us. It was a group of teenagers who were also going to the concert. They told me that the car's name was Sambo, and we drove the rest of the way with them.

We went to the Dead show. It was the most epic show. It marked a new era for the band, and their success only grew after this. We ended up staying there for four days. We didn't have anything to eat. It was wild. I remember Scott saying to me, "We gotta put this in a book."

And I laughed and said, "Yeah, we should put this in a book."

Anyway, we lived off drugs and partied. We maybe had a couple of oranges in those four days. But we did have a great time.

I never thought I was a rebel. I was just having fun as a teenager. My parents didn't understand. My brothers and sister were pretty strait-laced, so I was too much for them. I went to more concerts with my friends, Pink Floyd, and the like.

I came home from partying one day. My father sat me down and said, "I got something to tell you."

I was confused. He goes, "You're going to Utah. In two weeks."

I was sixteen. I went, "Where is Utah?"

He didn't reply. We didn't have cell phones back then, so I couldn't even Google where Utah was. I went to my friends and told them. We searched Utah on the map. It was out West, and I was surprised.

My parents were sending me to a Job Corp out there. They provide hands-on training and help people find a trade and make a career for themselves. This one was for maintenance. I needed this for my future, apparently. It was a six-month program, and I saw it as the end of my fun life.

I started partying with my friends even more. I had two weeks left. I wanted to make the best of them. I came back home the day before I had to leave for Utah. My father was appalled, but I told him I was ready. I packed my bags and was given instructions about the flight and who would greet me at the airport.

I did the program, I learned new skills. When I got out, being that I was a fast New Yorker, I didn't know how to relate to people my age. The kids there hadn't done any of the things I had. I found a place that served day-old cake for a quarter, and I used to bring it back to the dorm and sell it on credit. I would charge a dollar for it. I sold the cake, bought weed, and sold weed to keep the party going. I sold the drug and the munchies. I would walk around with my pockets full of money on payday, the youngest on the campus, and the most successful.

During this time, my friend from home (the one who was sent to hobo lane that day in church) was sent to Utah with his brother. They joined the Corp, and I showed them the ropes. We all started making money, and we started hooking up with girls. We were too young to book hotel rooms, so we had to ask an older guy to do it for us. We brought over two girls to the room, and some white guy answered the door. We got scammed by the older guy. He told us the wrong room number and kept our money.

We got tricked. Defeated, we went back to the dorms. I was supposed to go home soon, and I wanted to do something before that. I was upset. We saw that older guy on campus, and we beat him up. That was how we got kicked out of the Corp. We were sent home. The bus ride was two and a half days.

The crazy part is I was fortunate. I was allowed to graduate. I got my money. I got the certificate. I always thought I had a guardian angel watching over me.

I was back in New York. I went to school, and people looked at me like I was something strange. I got bigger, and people were intimidated by me. I kept on selling weed, skipping school. I hung out with a lot of white guys, which was how I met my good friends Tippy, Jojo, Chris, and Jack. We partied and went to rock and roll concerts, sold drugs… you know, teenage stuff. I remember Chris had money, or his family did. His mother would give him money for Christmas gifts, and he would give it to me. I used to go to the store and steal gifts. I'd give him the gifts and keep the money.

I had an aunt named Gladys. She was unlike my mother: warm and accepting. She was very special to me because she never made me feel like there was something wrong with the way I was. I used to be one of her favorite nephews and I could do no harm when it came to Gladys. I got a call from her one day. She was haphazard, talking about a squatter or something. I was confused and I asked her what she meant. It seemed that my parents told her to call me because some squatters had gotten into her house. She needed my help to get rid of them.

This was amusing to me. I wanted to help, so I took Tippy with me and went to her house. I didn't know how I would get the squatters out but I knew that I had to be there for my aunt.

When I was seventeen, I used to sell hash, different weeds, and pills. One of the guys ratted me out, I think. The cops in the area knew my car because I had been driving the same thing since I was sixteen. The car was a dump that I worked on with my friends. We stole parts from all around and used them for my car. I built it up myself and got it to function. We made it look like new.

Some cops pulled over my car one day. They told me to get out, and I tried to slide out the other side. They grabbed my pants, but I managed to escape. I ran to the woods and threw the stuff there. They arrested me, and I asked for one phone call. I called my father and asked him to put my dresser in the shed. It was full of drugs. He got rid of it. And I got locked up.

My friends put up bail money for me. Before I got out, the inmates in the jail made me a big birthday cake because I just turned eighteen. These were people I didn't even know.

When I came home, my father had packed up all of my stuff. "You can't stay here," he said.

I moved in with Maria, this little Italian lady who was always kind to me. I didn't have a job, but I had money from my businesses. I thought I would live that way for the rest of my life. I always gave Maria some money. She had seven kids of her own, but she took me in. I moved here and there, but she always had a place for me.

A funny thing happened during this time. I was in White Plains, staying with Maria at the time, I stole some umbrellas from Macy's. The security guard saw me. He started chasing me, and it went on for a while. I got tired, and I threw the stolen umbrellas back at him. He continued to chase me, and soon I was on Main Street, all the way to Battle Hill. It was snowing that day, and there was no way I could run up that hill. I saw the bridge before the hill and jumped over it, right into the water.

It was freezing. But I stayed put. All the cops wondered where I went. They looked for me on the bridge, but I was hiding under the water. I couldn't go to jail again, so I dealt with the cold.

They were finally getting ready to leave when all of a sudden, one cop goes, "Wait, wait! I see something!"

There was a flash in my eye: the light was pointed at me. "There he is," he said. They pulled me out of the water and started scolding me. "Are you crazy? You could freeze down there."

I spent that day in the hospital. The cops were nice; they even asked where they could get some dry clothes for me. I told them about Maria, and they went to her house. They knocked on her door and asked if she knew a Samuel Nisbett.

"Yeah," she replied. "He's my son."

The cops looked at her, a small Italian lady, and wondered how a big black kid could be her son. It was comical.

They told her what had happened, and she cracked up. She knew what I would get up to, so she laughed and gave them my clothes. The cops didn't even charge me that day. They were so amused. "You're nuts," one of them said to me at the hospital. "You're crazy."

Months after this incident, I was walking down the same street where I was chased. Every time a cop would catch sight of me there, they would crack up laughing.

I lived with Maria for a while before she moved to Florida. But she didn't like staying there. She moved back to New York in '79, and she had this beautiful apartment back in Florida. She told me I could have it if I wanted.

So, at nineteen, I jumped on a plane and ran to Florida. I took over the apartment. I had this three-bedroom co-op, and I started working in construction. I like to say that I'm the original person who started Airbnb because I rented the apartment out to all my friends from New York. They would come down, and we partied like old times. I should've patented it.

This didn't last, though. I got into a bar fight, and cops got involved. We fought with them, my friends and me. I started throwing stuff at them, I got crazy, and I got locked up again. Nobody pressed charges, so they let me out after forty-five days. But the cops were on top of us. I had been there for two years, but I got into too much trouble. I came back to New York.

I couldn't stay with Maria. She was in Harrison, NY, where all the white people lived, and I couldn't go there. I was homeless in New York for a while. I lied about having a girlfriend out of town, but I slept on a box in a staircase of a parking lot every night in White Plains, nestling a bottle of liquor. But I continued working. I saved up until I was able to get a place. I never gave up; it wasn't in my nature. I was a survivor.

CHAPTER THREE CHAOS

"Our real discoveries come from chaos, from going to the place that looks wrong and stupid and foolish."

— *Chuck Palahniuk*

Things started to get messed up even more. I was getting older, and my activities were getting riskier. I found myself caught up in a situation that would change my life. I was always in a haze, consumed by the streets, consumed by drugs and a desire to be free. I was abusing substances from the moment I woke to when I fell asleep. Days, weeks, months passed by, and I found myself living my life as an outsider. I could see what was happening around me, but I rarely felt it.

I was wobbling down the street one night, completely wrecked and in a stupor. I was high on angel dust, stuck in a bizarre accumulation of thoughts and regrets. I don't remember it well, but I do recall the sharp gust of wind that propelled me forward, the side eyes from passengers who saw me stumble, and the exhaustion of being alone.

I saw something ahead of me. A group of guys, not much older than I was. They looked dangerous, daunting, and upset. I wasn't worried about them coming at me. My brain wasn't working properly. Whatever happened next came to me in a flash: I remember them coming closer, I remember being told to put my hands up. They wanted something from me, but I don't recall what. Money? Weed? I wasn't sure. I shook my head, and tried to get by. One of the guys stopped me and then all hell broke loose.

I'm not sure who threw the first punch. My fist hit the guy in the face and I heard and unnatural crack coming from his jaw. Suddenly, the other guys were on me. Despite them being older, I was bigger than them. I thought this would give me an advantage. I tackled them, and tried to beat them one by one. There were too many of them, and I realized it too late. In an attempt to save myself, I started to run.

I ran across the street in the cold night, rushing forward without a sense of direction. My vision was blurred and my breath hitched at the back of my throat. I could hear them running behind me, getting closer. I found myself in front of a building, the door slightly ajar. Without thinking, I ran it and bolted the door behind me.

They slammed their bodies against the other side of the door, trying to get me to come out. But I stayed put, back against the frame, trying to sober up and breathe normally. When their voices subsided, I thought I was out of danger. I tried to gather myself, but just then, I heard noises coming from the stairs. Someone was already in the building.

Before I could run out, a man came running down, a hammer in his hand. He was yelling at someone to call the police and warned me to stay back.

I was still hazy but I could hear an Irish accent. I put up my hands and tried to explain to him that I ran in there by accident.

"Thief!" he screamed, swinging the hammer around. "Stay away! Police are on their way."

I shut my mouth, not wanting to make the situation worse for myself. If the police were coming, there was nothing that could save me.

I was cuffed in the next fifteen minutes, read my rights, and taken to the back seat of the cop car. This was when I noticed that I was bruised: my lip was cut open and I had a gash in the side of my head. I didn't remember being hit that badly. I was afraid, shivering from the adrenaline and cold, and I was alone. I didn't know if I would be incarcerated and I couldn't bear the thought of going to jail.

I tried to explain to the cops that I didn't steal from the Irish family. I tried to tell them that I was running away from a fight. But my appearance didn't help my case, and no one took notice of my requests. I got locked up that night and I didn't know if I would make bail. I didn't know who to call either.

After I got locked up, I stayed in Rikers Island for a few months. It was lonely and I needed something to fill my time. They put me in the dorm where I was able to cook for the correction officers. It filled my time while I stayed there, lamenting at my fate.

There was only one person I could call. My friend Liz was a constant source of support. She had Puerto Rican and Italian parents, which meant that she was upfront and feisty from the start. She was attentive and funny and she called me every day when I was incarcerated. Liz found a way to put up bail money for my release.

It took more than two years to fight my case. I struggled and went back-and-forth from court to prove I was innocent.

During this time, I decided to go to Florida. Liz was living there and I needed to be around someone who cared about me. Prison had hardened me and alienated me from my own mind. But Florida didn't save me. Crack was very available in state. As soon as I arrived, I could smell it in the air. I was smoking crack every morning, cooking in different hotels, and selling when I could. If we didn't have money, Liz and I would sell our blood for food. Life became crazier than I expected.

Benjamin Darconte, Liz's father, was aversive to me. Her father was Italian. He was a very nice man but, in the beginning, he didn't care for me. It wasn't until he found out that Liz and I were only friends. We were never intimate. Liz and I shared many apartments and stayed roommates and friends. We lived in New York and Florida. On July 7t, 1981 Liz was blessed with a beautiful daughter. She named her Lindsey. God deleted Liz from my life but not from my heart. The lessons I learned from this friendship and its loss... I could write an entire book on them.

One day I had to go to court. I had no money but I had a car (unregistered, totally illegal). I had twenty dollars, and a bag of coke. Back then you didn't have to pay for your gas up front. So, I would pump gas and drive off before paying. I made it all the way from Fort Lauderdale to New York in twenty-two hours, with an illegal car and no money in my pocket. Looking back at it now, I really believe I had a guardian angel watching over me. I had an 18B lawyer which meant that I didn't have to pay for his services. He was very good and worked hard to have me acquitted. It took a while, but I finally beat the case.

It was time to go back to New York and life resumed its course. We used to go to a club called *The Lollipop* in New Rochelle. You could have all the liquor you could drink for ten dollars. Chris and I went to a babysitting job, drank a big glass of Hennessy, and then went to the bar to party. A wild night ensued. I was so drunk that all I remember is waking up in the hospital room. There was no memory of the previous night. The doctor in charge informed me that I got into a fight with some guys at the club. Apparently, they kicked my teeth out.

I could have laughed from the pain. This did not slow me down. Nothing did, in fact. I used to believe I was indestructible.

I wanted to make more money. I wanted to do more drugs. So, I got together with a good friend of mine and came up with a plan. This was the buddy I used to go to church with. Our idea was to rob drug dealers. It was a bit ridiculous. I guess we were trying to clean up the streets and make money at the same time. It was almost as if I was Robin Hood: I used to rob stores, bread shops, milk trucks, and the likes and give what I had to poor people. There was a restlessness inside of me that wanted to help. It was good, but I was just going about it the wrong way.

My life was about to change. I had a friend, Rodney, who went to church regularly. He wasn't close minded, like most religious people I knew. He was calm and sweet. I liked that about him. One day, Rodney asked me if I would go to church with him. It was a strange request. I wasn't the kind of guy one would find at a church. In fact, I was banned from the one my family went to. The church opposed of me, that's what I thought. It was not meant for me. Community, tradition, and family were not mine to have.

But that day, for some reason, I agreed to go with him. It was refreshing, watching the community come together, their views and values aligned. It was something I had never seen before, at least, not in my own community. I saw religion as something that restrained you, and limited you. But those people, they looked happy and free. There was a glow about them, a spin in their step, and laugh in their pain. Rodney watched me when the preacher spoke, when the hymns were sung. I had never been so quiet. My heart was full, and I was overcome with a sense of being. I didn't realize it, but this would be the turning point in my life.

    Samuel Nisbett was about to be reborn.

CHAPTER FOUR NAVIGATION

"True navigation begins in the human heart. It's the most important map of all."

— *Elizabeth Kapu'uwailani Lindsey*

Rodney never really forced me to attend church with him. Although he would constantly nag about his church and tell me how much peace had come into his life because of the church, he always left my decisions to me. Whenever he would ask me to join him at the church, I would straight up refuse him by saying that Church was not a place where I belonged; it was only bar and partying that brought me happiness.

But, as they say, God knows the best. I witnessed the same situation. Despite being the kind of person who always avoided going to church and the one who was always into drugs and alcohol, I walked again into the church. I believe Rodney had some covert mission to take me back to church. It was he who told me that they had 6 days at church, and he wanted me to pick one day that was convenient for me to come and attend the prayers.

At that time, I thought I was doing it all for Rodney and to make him happy, but later I realized God made me do all this. It was He who called me back to the place from where I was once kicked out. Even though I had done many things against his teachings and drowned myself in sins, he still loved me. He wanted me to show up at the church and get my life on track.

Finally, it was the day for me to attend church again. After so many years, I was walking into the church with many different emotions. I was scared, nervous, and anxious. The flashbacks of the time when I was thrown out of the church were constantly playing in my mind, but I tried hard to suppress them.

As I walked up the stairs, I saw a big and beautifully lit hall right before my eyes. There were benches placed on both sides of the hall on which people were sitting and chanting in low voices. When I looked at these people, they seemed very friendly to me. They had bright smiles on their faces and their eyes had a distinct spark. The glow on their faces showed the peace they had in their hearts. As I walked through the narthex, I felt as if all those people were welcoming me with open hearts.

During the whole prayer, I remained seated there quietly. I was trying to soak everything and live the moments I had never really experienced previously. It was all very new and calming for me. I could experience the rebellious fire in me slowing down and my mind finally thinking about something apart from drinks and parties.

Something about it made me come back the third time. As I walked into the church and sat on the corner bench, an old woman came up to me and said,

"Son, I have been watching you."

I looked at her with a blank look on my face. I did not understand how she recognized me among 200 other people. It was hard for me to process that although I had started coming to the church a few days ago, people were able to remember my face.

At that point in time, I was still fighting my addiction. The church was helping me save my soul, but I didn't commit to it fully for almost a year because I was still wondering why these people were being so nice to me after all the awful things that I had done in my life. But, one thing that took me again to the church was their constant efforts to make my soul pious enough so that it could make it to Heaven.

At last, it was time for me to graduate from NA and come out as a clean individual. I was both happy and excited about it, so I decided to celebrate that event of my life. Pastor's son Jonathan accompanied me to the celebration of my being clean over drugs for one whole year. It felt as if I was yet again breathing into the fresh year like a free bird. There were no chains of addiction attached to me, and I could do whatever I wanted to do. Finally, there was only contentment and peace in my heart.

I went to church that Sunday, as clean Samuell. I walked up to the pastor to take his blessings when the first lady standing at the back of the church came to me and bumped her fist with mine.

"Oh boy, I heard you celebrated one year clean of drugs! That's great. But you did not invite me to your celebration."

The only reaction that I had at that moment was, "Wow!"

I was very happy to know that everyone in the church considered me as their brother or son. They showered me with so much love that I thought I didn't even deserve it.

But going to NA changed everything in my life. It made me realize that I could have fun without getting high or drinking bottles of alcohol. My life began to seem a lot easier and more peaceful once I got rid of my addictions. I got to know how it feels to be able to go out of town and relish like other normal human beings.

My life was getting on the right track. After dealing with my addiction and eliminating it completely from my life, it was time for me to find a decent job. I don't really recall when and who taught me this lesson, but I was told to always keep a job. Therefore, in the year 1993, when I was working at juniper hill elementary school in Greenburg as a chef, I tried to find a job that paid well and also offered a good position.

While I was still working at Juniper Hill elementary school, there, one of my coworkers told me that there was a girl, in the school who had the same surname as me. Since I knew that I had a very unique surname and it was very unlikely that someone else apart from my family would have the same surname, I understood that the girl was somewhat related to me. When I saw her, I instantly recognized that she would be my niece, but sadly, it wasn't my place to tell her that I was her uncle.

On rainy days I used to draw pictures of these young students and they would applaud my talent. I still remember these children would say, "wow, Chef Sam is such an Artist". Their praise would always bring a smile to my face and motivate me even more to draw.

One day, my niece came to me to get her drawing made. I drew her picture and she said, "Thank you chef Sam". Definitely, it was hard for me to not tell her that I was related to her but I had no option. I had to hide my identity. That was a hard pill to swallow but I kept on pressing on.

While I was navigating and trying to find a better job, I went to White Plains medical center and asked them if they had any openings for the position of chef. They replied to me within a few days and told me that there was no vacancy for the position of chef, but they were ready to hire me as a dishwasher. At that point, I was not in a position to say no to that job, so I immediately accepted it.

After working as a dishwasher for 2 weeks, I was promoted to a cook. It was only God behind all this, and he was making my way easier. He was giving me everything that I wished for and was protecting me from sorrows. I believe He was waiting for me to take one step toward him, and he would shower me with all the blessings of this world.

CHAPTER 5 DELETED

"This exile is a fascinating symbolic act from our modern psychoanalytic viewpoint, for we have held in earlier chapters that the greatest threat and greatest cause of anxiety for an American near the end of the twentieth century is not castration but ostracism, the terrible fate of being exiled by one's group. Many a contemporary man castrates himself or permits himself to be castrated because of fear of being exiled if he doesn't. He renounces his power and conforms under the great threat and peril of ostracism.

— Rollo May

At a very young age, I was deleted from a church. But I wasn't deleted from the love of God.

When the pressure of life got too bad, my higher power (which I call God) always worked it out for me. I lost my spiritual and natural family. At least, some of my natural family. The White Plains Deliverance Center became my family. They became the ones I could count on. I lost two brothers but I was blessed with a lot more. One brother that stands out was Ray Blake Junior. Yes, he was the reverend's kid, and he was human. Yes, the pastor wanted the best for him because he was the oldest son. Ray

Junior went through his ups and downs, but thank God he was never deleted from the church like I was when I was younger.

He knew what I was going through. He was always there for me. He tried to help me with my drug problems and any other issues I had. He was always there beside me. I remember I used to run the song service during this time. I did devotion and I used to get up in front of the church and sing hymns. I recall breaking down crying because singing the old spiritual hymns was too overwhelming.

"Can't nobody do me like Jesus, can't nobody do me like the Lord... He picked me up and turned me around, he's my friend... He healed my body and told me to run on, he's my friend, how can you not cry..."

I had to be a stronger person and lead devotion. In one song all I said was, "Yes Lord!" It shifted my perspective, my mindset, my life.

I thought all that I went through in my life was now my testimony. It was such a powerful song. We had service two times on Sunday. One day I went to the morning service and I said to myself, "I'm coming back to the night service."

I felt something within me. A force that pulled me in, lulled me, and soothed me. I wanted to hear it. I wanted to be consumed by it.

But when I went home and saw the guy that sold me drugs, it was a fight for me. I was trying to stay away from drugs and spend time in church, but the devil had other plans. I ended up getting a bag of angel dust. I smoked it but I still wanted to go to church.

When I got there, my brother Ray was on the drums and he saw me in my condition. He came to the back and whispered in my ear, "At the end of the service put your offer in and just leave. Don't say nothing to nobody."

I was grateful that I had a brother like Ray at that time. He didn't want to put me through something humiliating, something that would lower people's opinions of me. I'm so grateful that God is a God of second chances. Ray would tell me, "Brother Sam, no matter what, always keep coming back to God. It's gonna work out."

Ray was in one ear and his dad was in the other one. The rest of my spiritual family was there also. They helped to revive me and give me strength and a new life. They saved me and welcomed me when I was at my lowest. I remember the kindness of their words, the ease of their generosity, and the warmth of their smiles. In fact, I recall bits and pieces of what was said to me. No matter what I did, they loved and accepted me with open arms.

By this time, I had built so many bonds with different people. Charles was one of them. One of the kindest souls I have ever met, Charles was dearer to me than my own life. He was down on his luck when he came into my life. We got to talking, and we saw that life had handed us the same cards. We were afflicted by the world. He understood me and I him. We started to live together.

The co-op was named Windover Woods, located in Greenberg New York. I was fortunate to have access to this condo, where we moved in shortly after. It was a sweet little place. We supported one another through our lowest moments. The co-op was like a little community of nice people. We had a lot of friends there. I remember Allison and Felicia, coming into our apartments, laughing and sharing stories. We were like a big family, always there for one another. We would go to their houses too and hang out until the night became quiet. I had this glass dish on my table for cakes and every week I would make a new cake. My friends would come down and wonder what kind of cake I had prepared for the week. It is still one of my fondest memories. I also had a lot of animals that I cared for. I had a tarantula and a 55-gallon fish tank with all freshwater sharks. That was our home, Charles and mine.

Later, Charles met Nancy and moved in with her. She was someone who completely pulled him out of the darkness. She loved him the way a man deserves to be loved. I was happy for them. But tragically, I couldn't see them be happy for too long. When Charles died, I was heartbroken. I gripped away at every moment, every conversation I had with my friend. The devastation took over me and crippled me for quite a while. I still pray for Charles, wherever he may be.

More than this, the ache of losing Tippy was another hurt I feel to this day. Tippy was my childhood friend. He was Irish and

German, and an addict like I was. I lived with him for six years and built a strong bond with his mother as well. We were like brothers, tough and wild. But our friendship was imbalanced, and I fear that Tippy held me responsible for it. My return to God and religion made Tippy upset. He couldn't understand the change in his friend. I don't blame him: I barely recognized myself. So, he asked me to leave without informing his mother. And I did leave, without any fight, because we both chose different paths in life. I had to accept that. But I still loved him.

  Tippy was like a brother to me. It was really hard for me to imagine life without him and then I had to go through it. Sometimes we would go down to Harlem to get our goodies, at least that's what I considered goodies at the time, and that was when I felt the most at peace. People would look at us funny, and I would wonder why. I forgot he was white and in Harlem he stood out, but to me, he was just my brother. Like I mentioned before, at one point in my life, I was homeless and I didn't really have anywhere to go, I was living from place to place. Tippy told me I could stay with him and his family. I realized we were close, but I didn't see how I was going to stay with his family. I didn't even know his family like that. I was unsure about it. One day he brought me over to his house and I sat down and I met his dad. We had a discussion and his father said, "Sure you can move in."

It was so casual, yet so significant. I moved into the basement and I realized that my guardian angel was once again looking out for me. I lived with his mother, his father, and his sister, Laura. They always treated me like their own. I remember my first Valentine's Day with the Roth family. At the top of the steps was a little box of chocolate with Tippy's name on it and next to it there was one for me with my name on it. Mrs. Roth never forgot about me: she treated me like I was her son. I will always remember how she taught me how to be true and how to love. Love is an action, a word; love is a choice and a decision. Because your actions determine if it lives on or ends. Although Tippy, his father, and his mother have passed away, their love lives on in me. Tippy's death also left me inconsolable. We never got to reconnect. I never got a chance to show him who I had become.

People don't stay in your lives forever. But their impact is everlasting. I remember the people who have impacted me. They were the only forces that stood between me and my addictions. One of the counselors in the drug program I went to told me, "You walked 20 miles in the woods. You gotta walk 20 miles out." I wasn't sure if I understood this at first. But now I do.

What he was saying was if you did twenty years of drugs, it will take you twenty more to get it right. And I agree. I still haven't made it. But I'm on my way.

In the early seventies, I went to a vocational educational school called Educage, located in White Plains. This was a suburban city in Westchester County, situated by the little mall, which I don't think is there anymore. Back then, that was considered a big mall. Educage was a trade school for young people who didn't quite fit into the traditional school system. This school promised to teach us life skills that would allow us to delve into better careers and promising futures. There was a program called 'Scared Straight' hosted by a nearby local prison. Our school took it upon themselves to take us out to Rawway, a New Jersey State prison, so they could prevent us from stumbling on the path to becoming criminals. They didn't want us to end up behind bars.

I remember that day I took some Valium to help me calm down. I think I was too calm at the time compared to the others accompanying me through the program. A Jamaican guy was so nervous and scared to do the program that he made the entire bus stop and dropped him off in the middle of the road. He would have had to walk back home because there were no Lyfts, no Ubers, and no cell phones. But he was too scared of what was to come.

I recall going into this big maximum prison, above twenty prominent inmates. They told us to take off our shoes, but at the time, I was plodding. The prison smelled dingy. It was too early. We were there on a school day, and I felt hazy. We were among the first groups to experience a program of this nature. The inmates were there to intimidate us. But I wanted to be tough. I promised myself, *Next time, I'm going to be quick.*

They got in my face, and when they were talking to me, the spray of spit flew into my face. I was agitated. I wanted to fight back. Still, I knew I was a little dude; they could thrash me around. These guys were massive. I couldn't do anything, but I was thinking, *Man, I wish these guys, my friends, would join in with me.* But they didn't. The program was only for a day. It showed me what life could be like if I did not turn myself around and tried to be serious about my future. It stuck with me.

Fortunately, I never ended up in a situation like that. This experience deleted a lot of thoughts from my mind and calmed me down as a person in general. It made me think about how my actions could have lasting consequences.

My wild thoughts were deleted.

CHAPTER 6 SEARCHING

"If I cease searching, then, woe is me, I am lost. That is how I look at it - keep going, keep going come what may."

— Vincent van Gogh

Life is like a puzzle. It has so many pieces. Pieces like support, emotion, growth, happiness, God, family, and finding true love. I was searching for all of this.

It was 1995. I was so happy being in the church. I was safe and I was still searching. I went to see my mother and father and they weren't home. So, I asked a neighbor if they knew what time my mother would return. The neighbor said, "I didn't know they had another son. I thought they only had two sons."

I showed her my ID and she was so shocked to know that they had another son and a daughter. I waited at her house and when my parents came to the yard, she said she had a surprise for them. They were surprised, but they were not happy. My mother grabbed me, dragged me into the house, and told me to sit down. "You know you aren't supposed to come over here."

But I was so happy. Because I was back with God and I was living for the Lord. I felt that they would be happy for me too. But it didn't go that way. I couldn't show them, couldn't make them believe. How could I tell them I was happy? I was doing the right thing. They yelled at me at this point. I realized they still loved me. I know that sounds funny but that was the way I felt.

My father gave me a ride to the train station. He said, "Son, you don't realize. You are my blood. You're one of my most blessed children. Every night before your mother goes to sleep, she calls your name before God. She prays for you day in and day out."

That still didn't make me happy. But it did sound good. It warmed my heart.

I went to church the next Sunday. I sat down and talked with Rev Blake. I told him exactly what happened. I remember him leaning back in his chair, looking at me thoughtfully. He said, "Son, are you living for the Lord or for your family? What is your reason for living?"

"For the Lord," I said. "To make it to heaven?"

He said, "Don't worry. One day you'll be back with your family. Just as God makes little green apples."

I didn't believe him at the time but it did come true. I never stopped searching. After forty years, my brothers and I can say we are closer than ever.

In my search, I was fortunate to be an armor bearer for my pastor. I used to Carry his Bible. I used to work near the door of his office. If somebody wanted to come in, I would have to announce them. I was very fortunate because I was able to be by the

Reverend's side. I was working with a great man, a man of God. He had a lot of life experiences similar to mine. He presented me with encouraging words all the time. I was able to go on trips with him. We visited other churches. I was always by his side, learning about the Lord and about life. In my search, he was the greatest finding.

When he brought me to the White Plains Deliverance Center, located in Mt. Vernon, NY, I was changed. It consisted of a body of believers who endeavored to reach the lost at any cost. He gave me a spiritual family who loved me unconditionally, and in due time, God brought me back to my biological family. Forty years later, it was in his time. I pray for his soul daily.

In my searching for myself, and my family, I have a few people to thank. Every day I am grateful to God for David, my sister's husband. At one point in his life, he decided that my sister had to go. He met my mother and father during Easter. They had a conversation with him and it was decided that enough was enough. My brother-in-law took a stand back in 2005. On a Sunday morning, my sister came over to my house. Initially, I struggled to find an apartment in the city. But I managed to find a place near my mom, and it gave me the chance to reconnect with my family. I lived only a block away from my mother at this point.

My brother-in-law and sister lived in Virginia and stayed with me in New York, in a small part of The Bronx that my mother lived around. My brother-in-law stayed in the house, and my sister and I walked around the corner. My sister and I were holding hands. I remember that day like it was yesterday. There was light rain falling down. We were nervous.

I thank God that David took a stand. He had us go and visit our parents while we didn't know what to expect. They did welcome us in, wholeheartedly. That was the beginning of me finding another piece of my family. I was finally in touch with my parents again.

I was reconnecting with my family, bit by bit. They threw me a surprise birthday party. It was a beautiful change. I felt incredible and was thankful for the loved ones around him. I wanted that happiness, that contentment, to last forever.

In August 2006, my father got into an accident at the age of eighty-six. He fell and hit his head and was in a coma. I remember beings in the hospital room and my sister-in-law came in. She asked me who I was.

"Who are *you*?" I asked in return.

She said she was his daughter. I didn't understand this until later on. She was actually his daughter-in-law. I continued searching. We had to bury him on December 15. I remember when he was in the hospital, the nights spent by his side, and then going back to him after my shift was over. At that time, I worked as a cook at Serendipity in New York. My dad was in the ICU and I was able to go see him any time I wanted. One night I went there and the security guard told me, "You can't go see your dad."

I was going through so much back then. I didn't want to disrespect him. But I looked him in the eye and said, "Okay."

Then I kept walking. Nothing could stop me from seeing him. We barely had any time together.

I used to sit with him for hours. I just wanted to know that I was in his company. It was such a blessing. I remember one day when I went to the hospital and my mother was there. She asked me, "Why didn't you say hello to your dad?"

"Because he's in a coma," I replied.

"Come here," she told me.

She yelled very loudly and said my dad's name. His eyes popped open. I was so amazed by this. I didn't think that he would be able to hear my mother in that state. But they were married for fifty-four years. That was a lifetime of companionship. I guess you would hear anybody call you out of a coma if they knew you well enough.

My mom put my hand in his hand and said, "It's the baby. Squeeze his hand and let him know that you love him."

My father squeezed my hand. I was overcome with emotion. I remember going to the funeral. I saw my niece and nephew. I didn't even know them before. I could see in my niece's eyes that she wanted to say something to me. But she just didn't know how to go about it. My two older brothers lived up in Westchester and my mother lived right around the corner from me. I was able to tell them, that if they ever needed something they could ask me. This was another blessing, to be able to offer your loved ones something.

I said the same to my mom. "I'm right here," I reminded her.

Even if they didn't want to take the ride with me, this was still the beginning of my search. Whenever my sister had a little extra time, she always spent it with my mom. We were so happy to be reconnected with our family. After a while, my niece Jacqueline asked her father if she could contact me. She said, "Uncle Sam is in touch with Grandma. Why can't I get in touch with Uncle Sam?"

My brother didn't have an answer so he gave her my number. I had the opportunity to meet up with Jacqueline. We met at a Burger King in The Bronx on Jerome Avenue by my house. Jacqueline said to me that she hoped one day her father and I would get together and talk. She was so earnest in what she wanted.

I looked at Jacqueline like she had four heads. I said, "It is what it is."

She kept insisting. "No way that's gonna happen," I said.

My niece, however, felt a different way. She told me that her wish would come true soon enough.

And would you believe it? Today my brothers and I are best friends. God is so good.

God granted me all these things, and I didn't realize it. When I was younger, I thought I would find something incredible in my search. But I was on drugs. I had no idea what I wanted. My thoughts were very messed up and confused.

***

The weirdest thing happened to me one day. It was 1999, the edge of a new millennia, and I was still figuring myself out. I was driving around all sad in my light brown Chevy car. Even though I used to live up in Westchester, Greenburgh, I didn't like hanging in that neighborhood. I used to go down to the city to see what I could get into. I met up with these three very nice young ladies. I was a bit shy and had to work up the guts to ask them if they wanted to go to a local bar to have a drink. There was a nice place by Lincoln Hospital, in the Bronx.

At first, they refused because they didn't know me. So, I thought to myself, *If we got to talking for a little and get to know each other, perhaps something could happen?*

After some conversation, they took me up on my offer. There was one young lady who really stood out. She was beautiful in an effortless way. She had the prettiest brown eyes: she was smart, funny, and intense at the same time. I kept trying to get close to her subtly. At this time, I wanted to get the pretty young ladies drinks at the bar. When I got back, the one with the nice eyes refused it. Because she didn't see the bartender pour it. So, I had to go back up there and let her see the bartender pour her drink.

While we were at the bar, they played R&B and hip-hop. We talked and talked into the morning. When it was all over, the feisty girl gave me her number. Her name was Tyneki. I was over the moon. But I got fake numbers a lot, so I asked, "Is it real?"

She smiled. I was smitten.

To my surprise, the number was real. We stayed in touch with each other and we had a good friendship. But I was still running the street and acting like a jerk. Sadly, we lost contact with each other.

In 2007, I was living in the Bronx. My car broke down one afternoon. I jumped on the MTA bus to get home. The bus was very crowded and I bumped into a young lady. I didn't recognize her at first. But then I heard a voice say, "Oh? You can't speak?"

Low and behold! It was my good friend Tyneki. I was very happy. I also felt very silly because I didn't recognize her at first. I said to myself, *Maybe this is a dream.*

It wasn't. It was real and we got to spend time with each other. There is nothing like a good friend. Tyneki was pregnant. She told me how she was having a baby shower.

"That's nice," I said, smiling. "I'm a chef." I told her how I was also doing ice carvings and fruit displays. I also told her how unfortunately I lost my portfolio with all the pictures of my artwork. And she said why don't you just start a new one?

"Could you do one for the shower?" she asked me. And that will be the 1st picture in your portfolio.

That was no problem. I wanted to put out my best work for my good friend. I put my all into that fruit display. I made a baby carriage full of all kinds of fresh fruit. She was happy, and it filled my heart with joy to see her like that.

I was told when I was younger to be friends before lovers. Maybe that's what I thought I had with Tyneki. Yes, we had our ups and downs, but there were more good times than bad ones. On August 7, 2015, we went to Aruba and got engaged. We had a lot of fun in Aruba. We walked the beach like love was due. We went horseback riding and we were alone, just with each other.

Several years later we both lost our parents. We had each other's back and lifted each other up. When I lost my father, I took a picture of my whole family. I missed them so much and I didn't realize it. I blew the picture up very big and had it framed in my house.

Tyneki kept telling me to get back in touch with my family but I would tell her no. "As long as I have Brandon and Brenda," I used to say.

That's was all I needed for family. I was being hard headed. I thank God I had a woman who didn't mind speaking her mind. I was battling cancer as well but she was there. She kept me sane. She was my rock.

CHAPTER 7 I AM NOT TIRED YET

"Tired, tired with nothing, tired with everything, tired with the world's weight he had never chosen to bear."

— F. Scott Fitzgerald

Despite the difficulties I went through, I remained steadfast. I refused to bow down. It's as if I can't grow tired, not after everything I have triumphed over. The first time I went to Riker's Island, I was very scared. I had heard horror stories about the place, and I knew it was a notorious prison. I was worried that my father was still working there because I would have been very embarrassed to meet him in those circumstances.

I had been locked up for drug possession before, and I knew I needed to get my act together. That's when I met the counselor who introduced me to the drug program 'Vesid'. It was a tough program, but it helped me understand my addiction and how to manage it. I also got to meet some great people who were going through the same ordeal as me.

After completing the program, I knew I needed to do something with my life. I wanted to make a difference, to live better, to do more than just have time pass me by. I had always loved cooking, so I decided to enroll in culinary school. There was a joy attached to making something from my own hands, when I had known so little peace before this. The program was intense, but I loved every minute of it. I learned so much about cooking and the restaurant industry.

However, as much as I loved cooking, I didn't want to spend my whole life in the kitchen. There was not one part of me that wanted to be limited anymore. I wanted to explore other opportunities, so I decided to get a CDL license. Vesid supported me and paid for it as well. I was super happy when I earned my license. With my CDL license, I went to MTA for a job, but unfortunately, I was turned down due to my felony record. It was a devastating blow, but I didn't let it stop me. I returned to my kitchen job and continued to work hard.

I started working for *Great Performance*, a catering company in New York City. I loved the work, and I was grateful to have a steady job. Over time, I became an integral part of the team, and my hard work paid off. Now, I've been working at GP for twelve years.

Being that Great Performance was new, fortunately, we even had contracts all the way out in Miami. We had a contract with the Miami Open. They flew me there and I ran the burger stand. We did almost 2500 burgers a day. Not counting chicken sandwiches and chicken tenders. It was a lot of food. We did it very well. After I left the Miami job, I was able to go to Cuba with my sister, which was one of the most memorable times I had. We met our maternal family, and it was a life-changing experience. I had never met them before, and it was incredible to connect with my roots. The people, the culture, and the food were amazing. The journey uplifted my gratitude a lot.

Another unforgettable experience was when I visited Disney World with my fiancé and daughter. We celebrated my daughter's ninth birthday there, and it was magical. Seeing the joy on her face was priceless. It was a moment I'll never forget.

When I went to Disney World, I was very blessed. My cousin Diana gave me her timeshare for a whole week, which saved me money because I did not have to pay for a hotel. My cousin Jamal was doing his internship in culinary arts there. He took it up in college and he was able to give me a pass. I was able to go to two parks for free. We did three seminars and every time we went to one, we were able to get a free ticket for one person to go to a park. We all were able to go to another park for free as well. This trip was definitely another blessing. It was my guardian angel once again.

It was a humbling experience, and it made me appreciate the beauty of the world even more. I also visited Aruba with my fiancé, and we had a blast. We went snorkeling, explored the island, and enjoyed some much-needed relaxation.

More recently, I visited Africa, and it was an adventure of a lifetime. My trip to Liberia, West Africa, was basically a missionary trip. My niece Jacqueline was out there for six months helping out with a school. For her missionary work they gave her a house and I was able to live with her for ten days. I was able to bring stuff down from my church. What a blessing. I got to help out with the school supplies and I was able to bring other little items for assistance. I was fortunate to meet a very special young man named Kelly John. He helped me and showed me around. He was my right-hand man. I will always love him and I hope he knows that.

At this point in my life, I decided to change course and live my best life. I had to acknowledge that the way I was living was wrong and I had to go on a new Path. I had to decide I wasn't going to spend the rest of my life honoring people's expectations of me. A lot of running but I'm not tired yet. Sometimes you have to lose to win.

Looking back on my journey, I'm grateful for all the experiences I've had, both good and bad. They've made me who I am today, and I wouldn't be where I am without them. I'm proud of the work I do, and I'm grateful to have a supportive fiancé, son, and daughter. Life isn't perfect, but it's beautiful in its imperfections.

I remember back in the day there where always people in my life that I would try to show a better way. I remember taking my best friend Born/Frank to church with me. He would always say he didn't have anything to wear besides sweat suits. I told him that nobody would care about what he wore. I also told him that I would wear a sweat suit with him so he could feel comfortable. He was so worried about how he was going to look because most of the Men wore suits. There was a young Man at the church that told me to introduce him and Born/Frank so he could take him to purchase him a suit. The young Man ended up buying Born/Frank two brand new suits. At that moment I thought to myself this is Kingdom working! Me and Born/Frank went on a nine day road trip to Florida. One of the funniest moments about the trip was we stopped at a gas station in Alligator Alley. The station sold alligator bites. I suggested we try them. Born/Frank did not want to try the alligator bites. I told him that we only live once. We laughed and he decided to try them with me. I realized at the moment how good it was to see us both changing. Life was good! We were both striving to be better Men.

CHAPTER 8 THANKS

"We can complain because rose bushes have thorns, or rejoice because thorns have roses."

— *Alphonse Karr*

As I sit here reflecting on my life, I realize that I have been blessed to have so many incredible people come into my life and influence me in so many different ways. Each person has played a unique role in shaping who I am today, and I am forever grateful for their impact.

One of the earliest and most profound influences in my life was Reverend Ray S Blake. He was always there to counsel me and offer encouragement through his moral stories. His son, Reverend Blake Jr., also played a significant role in my life. I always considered him my big brother, and he was someone I could turn to for guidance and support.

Brother Hercules was another brother from church who I hold in high regard. His unwavering faith and dedication to his community were an inspiration to me, and I am grateful to have had him in my life.

My mother was also a constant presence in my life until the age of twelve. She never stopped praying for me and taught me a lot. I am still grateful for her support, even during the darker times.

Tippy's mother was another person who had a profound impact on my life. She taught me how to love and be kind, and I am forever grateful for her influence.

My brother, Steve, taught me a lot about animals and how one should keep pets. I am thankful for his presence in my life and how we reconnected.

Dr. Chest, a good acquaintance, and Johnson, who used to work with me at the construction job. While both men are no longer with me, I remember them fondly as friends. I was so upset with their passing that I went for a check-up. During this process, I was diagnosed with prostate cancer. This check-up might have saved my life.

Dr. Lerner, the man who did my surgery. I truly value his effort and am grateful to him.

I also want to thank my company, Great Performance, and the friends from there: Desmond, and Roland. And I can't forget the CEO, Liz. She's the sweetest person on earth!

I am grateful for all the drug programs I attended. especially, The Real Dad Network. It was instrumental in helping me be a better person. I would like to thank Samaritan Village, as an alumnus. Thank you.

In the end, I would like to say something. Life is like a book. Some chapters are sad. Some are happy sounds like excitement. But if you never turn the pages, you would never know what the next chapter would hold.

I want to thank everybody for reading this book. And being part of this book where I told my life story. I'm looking forward to eternal life, which is salvation. This book I pray that somebody reads it and realize that at the end of every tunnel is light. And I'm so glad that you were able to read this book. God bless you and have a nice day.

When I think of the goodness of Jesus and all He has done for me, all I can say is thank You. I can never repay You. One thing I can do is live my life before other men to show them how You brought me out of darkness into the marvelous light and how there is a better way to live: living for You. I'm also grateful and would like to thank the late Reverent Harry Fuller and Sister OE Blake, Brother Bobby L and Brother Knot, and so many more. I also want to thank a few men and women that are still on the battlefield: Bishop J Gregory Thorpe, Lady Vancy Thorpe, and Reverend John Tyer.

Tell me how do you handle the guilt of your path? Tell me how do you deal with the string and how can you smile when your heart has been broken and is full of pain? Ron Winans said in his song, "All you gotta do is stand..."

In memory of my best friends.

Liz

My brother Tippy & Me

Charlie.L

Chris and Tippy

My dad awesome baking skills.

Learn more about me In the kitchen.

Sam Nisbett
   Chef San Nisbett feutured...
   www.youtube.com

My family

Aunt Gladys

God is good

God said, "You are different. I did not create you to fit in. I created you to stand out."

Rev. Ray S Blake.

Christ is the answer

Olive Nisbett (Mom)

Made in the USA
Middletown, DE
14 April 2024